Vitan Flourishing
Living Large Without
Guy Lane

Chapter 1

You have everything laid-out perfectly, but something's not quite right.

It works for you. It works for your guests. But someone is excluded.

Not someone. Something.

It's the insight that your life doesn't exist without context.

You are a thread in a tapestry.

But the tapestry is fraying.

You are not the cause of the fraying. But you are a cause of the fraying, and you will be a victim if it unfrays further.

And then you brighten as you remember that every cause of fraying can be a cause of unfraying.

So, let's unfray together.

That's a new word: fraying.

A new idea.

New words can be scary because they ask us to question the old.

But we should embrace new words, because we can't unfray without a new language.

Here's a new phrase: Vita Sapien.

What a pain in the ass. Seriously.

"What does that even mean?"

It's Latin for *Life Wise*.

"So, I should learn Latin, now? Why don't you just call it Life Wise?"

Because that's a brand of dog food.

"*Ahhh.*"

It's a highly contested market-space of brands, names, and ideas out there.

Getting something through the noise is hard.

Most of what comes through the noise wants you to buy something. Generally, something made of petroleum oil.

That's our system. And it works! For them.

And if it keeps working, we all slide into the hot abyss.

You know that. You have known that for a long time.

But it's complicated. Gloomy. A real party-killer. So we don't talk about it. We just let the thought slip away.

Well Vita Sapien—the pain in the ass—has something for you.

The hot abyss is for losers.

We are going to the Verdant Age., instead.

Let me explain what that means Vita Sapien's bamboozling language, that no one really understands:

The Verdant Age is the potential future time when humanity and the Living Planet thrive in synergy deep into the Long Future.

What does that mean? Who wrote this. Who dreamed this stuff up?

Every civilization has a complicated language that underpins it. You don't have to learn it. You just need to trust it makes sense.

But what does it mean?

It means you need a scooter.

And some PV.

Chapter 2

So, we are going to the shop to buy some milk.

Cow milk. Really?

Have you read what they do to cows?

How about, instead almond milk. Soy milk. Oat milk. There's a ton of options now.

But what's the difference?

Ahhh?

Ask your friends. Someone will know.

And what's you frame of reference for choosing milk? Health? Cost? Impact on the tapestry of life? What do you actually care about when you buy milk?

And here's the thing.

The best thing for the tapestry of life is that you don't buy milk. Because milk needs to be made. And making has a footprint.

Seriously. Put the milk money in a tin for another use.

So you let the idea of having milk in your coffee slide, and choose to drink your coffee black.

And you are surprised because less is often more and you say, *"Hey, this black coffee has a character of its own."*

But you are still hankering to go to the shop. For personal reasons ;)

"Do I walk?" Great idea. "*Ahhh.* That's twenty minutes each way. It's hot. I'll sweat. And I'll have to change after."

Drive?

Sure, let's drive. What a great idea. Let's consume petroleum hydrocarbons to move a 1,500kg car made of metal and rubber and plastic, and then prowl around forever trying to find somewhere to park.

Here's a better idea.

Take the scooter.

It's plugged in. You have solar, so it is charged up with fresh energy delivered daily. There and back it consumes barely a bees-dick of electricity. Just a whisper of solar electrons.

You can zoom past the boring bits of the journey and step off to say "Hi" at any point on the way.

You see, the world is changing. And if you change too, it's all good.

You can live large without.

Without?

Without arduous toil. Without spending money. Without putting poison in the air. Without feeding cashing into industries that are destroying the tapestry of life.

That's the game you should be playing. It's called Vitan Flourishing.

It's got new words and new ideas.

Like, when you live without, you have more to do with.

Chapter 3

Vita.

That word again.

Vita Sapien. Vita Flourishing. Vitan Chique, Vita Sobriety, Vitan Meditation.

The list goes on.

So what is Vita?

Vita is Latin for Life.

Vita is a movement to preserve Life on Earth.

Vita Sapien is the name of a philosophy—a sustainable life philosophy.

It's also the name of an organisation —an Australian registered charity— that advances the philosophy.

This book is published by Vita Sapien Organisation.

Vita Sapien was conceived in October 2016.

The insight was that the climate and ecological crisis that grows everyday isn't caused by economics or politics or technology.

It's primarily caused by people holding unsustainable beliefs—that's why we are okay with unsustainable economic and energy systems.

The mainstream worldview leads us to pursue lifestyles that harm the tapestry of life.

So, the mission was to conceive a worldview that gave humanity the best chance of surviving the 21st Century and thriving beyond.

That's Vita Sapien Philosophy.

There's a little book.

But it's quite dense.

It's readily available, but not for everyone.

The book you are reading now about Vitan Flourishing introduces Vita Sapien Philosophy by talking about some of the lifestyles that stem for applying the philosophy in daily practice.

Regarding the milk, there are three wisdoms in the little story:

1. Be mindful about what you consume

2. For every purchase there is a purchase forgone

3. Everything has a carbon footprint, but somethings have none (practically none)

Vitan Flourishing is the idea that people can have full and vibrant lives without.

- Without a big environmental footprint that frays the fabric of life
- - Without the guilt that some lifestyles produce

- Without needing to have vast sums of money

- Without need to acquire vast sums of money—which generally means you have less time working and more time for things you love.

- Without buying things that you don't need or want

Vitan Flourishing lets you live large with less.

Lets' consider some of the other Vitan lifestyle elements.

Chapter 4

There is a concept called Simplification.

It means that the future is going to be simpler, whether we like it or not.

So best get ready.

Simpler means that supply chains will be disrupted.

Energy will be more expensive.

High consumption (normal) lifestyles will become harder to sustain.

Environmental footprint will be policed.

In France they have a word: *Sobriété.*

Another complicated word! What is it with these Vita Sapien people?

It means choosing to live simply.

Not because you have to, but because choose to because it is better. And because you will have to eventually because of simplification.

Let's tighten our belts now because we are going into hard times.

So, Vitan Sobriety is not about stopping drinking.

Vitan Sobriety is about choosing to cut back on consumption as a lifestyle that protects you from the future.

And Vitan Chique? What's that?

Vitan Chique is dressing well in second-hand clothes that have no plastics in them.

Nylon, polyester are out.

Wool, cotton, and natural fibres are in.

Vitan Chique: cost effective, stylish and sustainable.

You see, at the heart of the simplification and the climate and ecological crisis is plastic and fossil fuels—coal, oil and gas.

Plastics are made of oil and gas.

Our civilization has been gulping down fossil fuels for 300 years since the Industrial Revolution.

And we have practically bankrupted the *global ecosystem* from all the pollution, all the carbon in the air, all the plastic in the sea.

Global Ecosystem. Another new phrase. It means all the animals and plants on Earth that function to keep our planet habitable for life. We need them.

You exist because plankton make oxygen to breathe.

Fossil fuels are destroying the global ecosystem.

You want to know how much pollution fossil fuels produce: 50 billion tons.

Every year.

And plastic is everywhere.

Big pieces, small pieces. Pieces so tiny we breathe them in.

We now have plastic in our organs.

Plastic in our brains, and livers.

Plastic in the placenta and the baby in the womb.

New-borns enter the world *pre-contaminated*. That's a real expression.

It's time to stop this madness.

There's a cartoon on Facebook. A woman in a shop buying a fish for dinner. She says, "Can I have a bag?" The shopkeeper says, "Already inside."

Lol :(

It is time to let plastic and fossil fuels go the way of the dodo and the dinosaur.

We say, "Modern civilization was built by fossil fuels and plastic. But now they are killing everything.

Thank you for your service. You have to go now."

We will still need energy and materials.

But we can get these from other sources. Sources that are kind to people and planet.

To do that we need to transition.

Chapter 5

Transition.

Sounds like a type of make-up.

It's not. Its a change from one system to another.

It's inevitable. Its going to happen eventually whether we like it or not.

The public won't sit back and see their life support system being eradicated.

Fossil fuel are finished—renewables energy with storage is better. We just need to hurry it along. Before more people get hurt.

This is a difficult time, when a mature system is revealed to be toxic and deadly and it needs to be swapped with a new system.

The beneficiaries of the old system pressure the political class to give them favours and delay the inevitable.

Its the people and the planet who suffer.

And when the planet suffers, people suffer more.

There is something you need to know about this. A new word for you.

Don't worry. It's short. Just four letters:

Gaia.

Chapter 6

James Lovelock died in 2022 at the age of 103. He was an independent British scientist. Back in 1976 he co-authored a science paper with an American biologist called Lynn Margulis.

I won't tell you the name of the paper just yet because it will break the flow of this document.

I'll break it down word by word because the title is profound. It starts with the word *atmospheric*.

Atmospheric refers to the atmosphere, the bubble of gas that surrounds planet Earth. From the ground, it goes up to about 100 kilometres. Its very wispy up there, not much air. Close to the ground the air is thick, rich with moisture. Its the lower 10% where all the weather is. That's where you'll find humans except when they are flying in airliners.

The second word is quite complicated: *homeostasis*.

This means something that stays within boundaries. Like your refrigerator always stays around 4 degrees Celcisus.

So, *atmospheric homeostasis* means conditions in the atmosphere staying with in boundaries. What conditions? Temperature, mainly.

So, the next part of the title is: *by and for the biosphere.*

Another curly word: *biosphere*. Break it down to *bio* and *sphere*.

Bio means life. Sphere is a ball-shape.

And that's the shape of life on Earth. A thin sphere of living organisms in the ocean, the forests, the birds in the air. The biosphere is the *sphere of life* on Earth.

It extends from the bottom of the ocean to the top of the clouds. A maximum of about 30km.

Standing in a forest, the trees look huge, but seen from the moon, the biosphere is smaller than the atmosphere, that is just a thin veil of gas over our planet.

Planet Earth is about 14,000 kilometres wide. Around the edge just 100km of gas, and withing that gas the thin strip of life. The biosphere

So, the title is *Atmospheric homeostasis by and for the biosphere.*

It says that the atmosphere is being regulated to stay within narrow band of temperature <u>by</u> the biosphere AND <u>for</u> the biosphere.

The planet looks after itself. And its been doing so for over 3 billion years.

It's like when you get up from your seat to adjust the thermostat to make conditions more comfortable for you in the room.

Life on Earth regulates the temperature of the planet by manipulating the atmosphere on its own behalf.

Take a moment to ponder just how profound that is.

The last part of the title gives this phenomena a name: *the gaia hypothesis*.

A hypothesis is a theory that is not yet full substantiated. Years later, further research shifted the Gaia hypothesis to Gaia Theory, and later it became embedded in a broader scientific field called Earth System Science.

And Gaia? Well, that's the name of the ancient Greek Goddess of the Earth.

So, the full title of the paper is:

Atmospheric homeostasis by and for the biosphere: the gaia hypothesis.

This paper contains profound earth wisdom. Not ancient wisdom, but modern scientific wisdom.

It explains the mechanism of how Earth has sustained life for billions of years. The biosphere is a self-regulating sysem.

Atmospheric homeostasis by and for the biosphere: the gaia hypothesis

By JAMES E. LOVELOCK, Bowerchalke, Nr. Salisbury, Wilts. England and LYNN MARGULIS, Department of Biology, Boston University, 2, Cummington Street, Boston, Mass. USA

So, in short, the paper says that life on Earth has evolved mechanisms to ensure that the temperature of planet Earth remains within a narrow window—not too hot, and not too cold—to maintain an abundance of life on Earth.

How would it do that? There are lots of mechanisms, but none so fascinating as the way the plankton make the clouds.

Really? Plankton make the clouds.

Yes. And this is why Vitans say: "Thanks Plankton."

Chapter 7

The word plankton comes from the Greek root that means wanderer. These are (typically) tiny organisms that cannot swim against the tide, so they just drift. There are two broad types of plankton: plant plankton and animal plankton.

Technically, these are known as phytoplankton and zooplankton.

Vita Sapien calls them the Phyto and the Zoop.

The Phyto are the plant plankton. And these things are tiny. There are thousands of different types.

One type has a ridiculously long name. Let's break it down:

coco—litho—phore

Coccolithophore.

Each of these little round plants* is so tiny you need a good microscope to see them clearly.

* Technically, they are not plants, but algae. For our purposes, same same but different.

These things are tiny, that 10 would fit across the width of a human hair.

Anyway, despite being tiny, there are billions of them in the ocean.

And they produce a type of gas that rises into the air, breaks down in the presence of UV Rays and releases a tiny dot of sulphur.

In the air, water vapour—like humidity—forms on the tiny speck of sulphur and forms a water droplet. Trillions of water droplets form a cloud.

The cloud does two things. First, sunlight falling on the cloud is reflected back into space. So, the cloud keeping the surface of the ocean cool buy shading.

Secondly, the cloud drifts over land, rains and waters the crops that are our healthy food.

Furthermore, as the little phyto grows, it absorbs CO2 gas from the sea into its body.

CO2 contains carbon, so when the phyto dies, it sinks to the sea floor, taking the carbon with it.

In this way, the phyto move carbon from the air to the sea floor. This is important because too much carbon in the air makes the planet too hot.

And that's why Vitans say thanks plankton.

Chapter 8

But Vitans are also known to say, "Sorry, Plankton," in recognition of all the havoc we have caused on Planet Earth.

The Swiss organisation World Wildlife Fund releases a document called The Living Planet Report.

It says that humans have destroyed 70% of wildlife over the last 50 years. Another report says that if you weighed all the mammals on Earth, only 3% is wild animals, the rest is humans, our livestock and pets.

A Russian scientific finding shows that forests act as huge air conditioning systems called *Biotic Pump*. And yet forests are being smashed everywhere.

At some point, we humans need to wake up to the crisis that we have bought to the Living Planet.

You see, Gaia may have survived for over 3 billion years, but if we humans keep at it, she could die. She is already very sick.

And without the Gaia to regulate Earth's temperature, we will all perish soon after.

This is not a new concern. Scientists and environmentalists and others have been trying to get this message out for decades.

But now we are in the last years, months, weeks of being able to control our destiny on Earth.

We can't keep growing the global economy based on poisonous fuels that add heat trapping gases to the atmosphere.

We must transition. We must transition economically, technologically and spiritually.

On the seafloor, a SCUBA diver is at the whim of their gear. The tank, hoses, regulator, dive computer, fins, mask and weight-belt. Some pieces of kit are convenient, some are life critical.

If we humans are to stay on Planet Earth, we must treat our life support system—Gaia, the biosphere—with the same reverence as a SCUBA diver treats their kit.

At the heart of humans disregard for life on Earth is the spiritual philosophies that dominate the planet. Mainstream Religions and New Age spirituality are notoriously absent anything meaningful to say about life on Earth. Its all about life after death and crystals and yoga.

There is nothing wrong with these things, *per se*, but our civilization has slipped into global crisis and will slip over the edge to the hot abyss.

And this is where Vita Sapien comes in to make things right.

Chapter 9

Whether you are spiritually grounded by Jesus or Crystals or the Buddha, you will understand that we cannot survive unless we keep our Living Planet in tip-top condition. And to do that we need a new spiritual philosophy to augments those that exists today.

Vita Sapien advances Ecosystem Spirituality.

The word ecosystem describes the interconnections between living organisms and the physical world they inhabit. The biosphere is an ecosystem, the comings and goings in the garden pond is an ecosystem.

When we connect spiritually with ecosystems big and small, we develop moral concern for their wellbeing.

And that moral concern translates into actions that helps protect them.

Vita Sapien is a complete philosophical system that includes Ecosystem Spirituality.

It is believed that millions people will come to adopt Vita Sapien

Philosophy as their primary worldview.

The behaviour change that is triggered by this global transformation will be sufficient to drive the transition from the destructive uncaring world today, to the Verdant Age.

The Verdant Age is the potential future time when human civilization and the biosphere *thrive in synergy*.

Thrive means more than just surviving, it means flourishing—Vitan Flourishing.

And synergy means working together. We look after the

biosphere, and the biosphere looks after us.

At the heart of the global mass-awakening to the spiritual beauty of nature is Gya.

This is like Gaia the scientific theory, but Gya is a spiritual belief.

A spiritual belief that all life on Earth is part of a single being, and that we humans are cells in the greater body.

This gives us a special responsibility as we are wholly dependent on the health and wellbeing of Gya.

You are part of Gya, the biosphere.

So we should care for the biosphere.

And that means paying attention to what milk we buy and how we travel to the shop to buy it—the solar powered scooter, remember.

This, in its essence, is **Vitan Flourishing**.

Read the *I, Biosphere* poem, below.

Sit with the words for a while.

Then ask yourself, "What should I do with the rest of my life?"

I, Biosphere

I am human

I come from Earth

In a little bubble of gas

With molten lava below

The freezing depths of space above

I am one organism

Made of billions of organisms

Amongst trillions of organisms

In a vibrant community

A biological sphere of life

The biosphere

I am part of the biosphere

I, biosphere

You, also, are part of the biosphere

You, biosphere

We are all in this together

The humans and all else that lives
on Earth

We, biosphere

We are all part of the biosphere

And the biosphere is part of us

So, we should care for the
biosphere

We really can't live without her

oOo

What's Next?

When we identify as part of the biosphere, we begin to unfray and heal our beautiful Living Planet.

Learn about Vita Sapien, join a Vita Sapien event… and so much more:

vitasapien.org

Comments

This is a pass-around pocketbook.

Write your comments below and then give the book to someone, asking them to read the book, make a comment and pass it on to someone else.

If you are the owner of the book, maybe put your details below.

Name: ___________________________

Date:______________

Contact(optional):______________

Comment:______________

____

____

____

____

____

____

www.ingramcontent.com/pod-product-compliance
Lightning Source LLC
Chambersburg PA
CBHW011929050726
47591CB00009B/2404